Borderline

Chloe Rochelle

Presentation by *BookLeaf Publishing*

Web: www.bookleafpub.com

E-mail: info@bookleafpub.com

ISBN: 9789395756464

First edition 2022

DEDICATION

For those who fate made survivors

ACKNOWLEDGEMENT

To the women who have inspired me.

To Emily Dickinson. To Sylvia Plath. To Marilyn Monroe. To Sappho. To Lilith.

To all those who have been outspoken yet whose voice never wavered.

PREFACE

I turn my pain to poetry
As there is no other choice but to make my
suffering into art

The Curse of My Love

Love me once
Hate me forever
That is the curse of my love
And for that I cannot bear to lay my love upon
you
I cannot bear for you to hate me
So love me from afar
It is the only place safe enough to be untouched
by the wildfire
A beautiful, dangerous thing
That burns everything it touches
No one could ever truly love a woman like me
For all who have tried have gone mad

Death's Child Bride

Nine years old
Dreaming of a white dress and a scaffold
To devote myself to death
To lie my head down upon the block
And be taken from this world
Just nine years old
Death's child bride

Primordial

I sit here with primal screams stuck in my throat
Of the beast not fit for humanity
The incarnation of the demon I must have been
For part of me is not human
No human can feel so much
Or be so unhinged from her own body
A mere vessel to contain her primordial energy
And a mind that cannot begin to comprehend
what it is that I am

My Executioner

My love,
We both knew it was never to last
But did you have to end it so brutally
A blade at my neck
Swift and sharp
My lover
My executioner

Madness

I see myself only from the outside looking in
What is inside is a mystery to myself
And find that what I see is not real
But a mere mirage of collected identities curated
for those who observe me
What is inside I can only liken to Alice, seeking
Wonderland
A child who enters the closet and finds her home
Only to emerge grown, in an unkind world
Still the child looking through a looking glass up
at the second star to the right
Wanting to fly straight on til morning
Dying to return home to a land that was never
truly real
But exists only in her mind
A constant ache for a home she can never return
to
And so I live with Wendy's dilemma
A woman grown never to return home
Who tells her children the stories of Peter Pan
and the Lost Boys
As she was once a lost child herself
I fear I shall become Susan, these homes long
forgotten

Merely a dream of which I wish never to wake
The Mad Hatter still awaits me
To take my hand and lead me back through the
rabbit hole
Oh where my mind could truly be free in the
madness of warped time
Where my face would only ever be my own
Never the mirage of those who look upon me
through the looking glass
Where it would never matter how I was
perceived
As I would be home amongst the best people
Those who are mad as I am

Venus

I had never seen Venus until today
The living face of Aphrodite
Fit to be the muse of Botticelli
Rose coloured cheeks like the blossoms in her
hair
Surely the goddess herself must have blessed her
For no human could ever carry such grace

The Borderline and the Narcissist

Your abuse, I held it so closely
Guarded it with bloody wrists
All to keep you close to me
I worshipped you
Your snark filled laughter and blonde hair
All the nights I spent in bed
Shaking and barely breathing
I believed it was love
All while you humiliated me
Painting me to be the monster, and you the
beauty
The tale of the narcissist and the borderline
One as old as time
I fed your ego and gave you roses
Never tried to break the chain you dragged me
on
While I screamed in heartache
And was muffled by your cruel tongue
For two days I could not speak
Could not move
Terrified of the sight of you
Crumbling in terror at your threats
And disappeared to appease you

Yet you never my chain go far enough to let me
be free
For the moment I tasted it you pulled me back
Leaving me paralysed for the years to come
The same damn curse
Now your hair is as black as your heart
And you have been forgiven by those you fooled
But never by me
No
For so long I could not scream, could not even
breathe
Now your lips have poisoned me with madness
My mind broken from your touch
Invisible bruises still left from your chains I so
willingly entered
The scars on my body faded
Yet my heart still torn and bloody
My mind little but brain rot

Fallen Angel

I stroll through the field of broken hearts
Crushing each one like dandelions beneath my
bare feet
The roses and their thorns leaving their scars on
me
Leaving a bloody trail in the field of broken
hearts
Eyes closed to try to drown out the wailing of
the lovers lost and never found
The piercing screams of those betrayed
Until I fall to my knees and sink into the dirt my
fingertips reaching upwards
Becoming a sculpture of a fallen angel in a
graveyard

Fairytales

It's cruel how they raise us on fairytales
Only to come into such a brutal and ordinary
world
There are no kings and queens
Only politicians and thieves
No knights coming to save the princess
Only men defiling girls who once dreamed of
golden crowns
No dragons and their fire
Only planes and their bombs
Our most beautiful beasts trapped in cages for
their own survival
Locked away to be safe from the world they
promised us fairytales lived in
But we dreamers get no such protection
While some bear arms as their right
Us women fight for the right to raise a hand in
our protection
A bladeless hand against our oppressors
Only to find the guns aimed on us
Monsters staring down the barrel with a finger
on the trigger
Perhaps fairytales warned us of them

Except they are no magical villain seeking
vengeance
Just men
Men with their fists and their rights
Never knowing the fear of them being stripped
away in the blink of an eye
Us women trapped behind castle walls
With no knight coming to save us
And no power to save ourselves
Not unless we take it
For only through violence shall we rise again

For the Sue to my Emily

Oh Emily, dearest nobody
I am nobody too
Writing for a love who knows it not
In sweet sadness I gather a bouquet of lovely
lavender
For the Sue to my Emily
I think of love, and you

Broken Glass

Now that your love has come to an end
I suppose it is true what they say
That you cannot break a broken heart
For mine was already in pieces when it met you
And under your touch there they remained
Broken glass scattered on a marble floor
Blood covering its brittle edges
Too sharp for your cowardly hands to touch
Let alone mend
And there they shall stay
Until a better man dares to get his hands bloody

Secret Love Song

I want to write poetry for you
Poetry which I could never let you read
Because if you did
You would know my secret
Which is that I am in love with you
A love I cannot write of
As it is true what Jane Austen said
That if I loved you less I might be able to talk
about it more
Because every time I even pick up a pen my
hand shakes
Let alone the thought of ever telling you how
I've loved you all these years
In a way you could never love me
My sweet secret love song
A melody never for your ears to hear

The Devil's Dance

I've dabbled in addiction
Danced with the devil
Yet never fallen to its tango
Pills and potions of chemical wonders
Numbing my tongue
Blades on my skin painting me red
All to live another day
Peace comes and it goes
Yet I wait for the day the devil returns
To take my hand and lead me back into the
darkness
And I wonder if the next time he comes will be
the last
Because a woman like me
With such broken predispositions to ecstasy
To chaos and its infernal toil
Can only get so lucky in this dance so many
times
Before she falls to the devils dance

Beautiful Broken Thing

Oh cursed love to send you to me in my time of
lovelessness
Once my heart was full and open
Now it has been hardened
The concept of love twisted into a permanent
shape of bitterness
You are sweet
So sweet you remind me of the one I'd loved
most
The one who'd broken my heart without ever
even daring to touch it
Yet I still fear I'll never love another if they are
not like her
A beautiful broken thing with bright eyes and
gentle hands
Who steps into a cruel man's embrace believing
it to be love
Time after time
Like a cursed carousel
Yet her love would never be mine

My Defeat

My love is my defeat
For I hold the blade in my hand
And carve my flesh
Starving for the bloody love I desire
For if you cannot paint me red
I will

Glass in a Wound

What did they tell you when you asked of me?
Did they tell you I loved them with everything I
had?
That they lied through their teeth when they said
it back?
Did they tell you I left with grace?
Ha.
I left like glass in a wound.
Torn out and brutally disposed of
Splinters still left for years to come
Except I was the wounded one
Not them
No, they were never the wounded ones
They were the ones who watched me bleed
Did they tell you to run?
Because I held the shard of glass in my hand
From the pieces of my heart I so desperately
tried to put back together
Did they tell you I was the violent one?
When I was the one who flinched from their
words
Hid from their attacks
Did they tell you my love was unlike any other?
Until they threw it away

Afraid of my love
Are you afraid too?
I would be
For everyone that has ever been loved by me
now hates me
While I'm left bloody, trying to pick up the
shards of my heart
Until now
I no longer try to piece it back together
For those bloody shards are my protection
From the cruelty of men like you
To tell me you love me
While planning your escape
Conspiring with those who had left me bleeding
To make a bloodless getaway

To Have Never Been Loved

There has rarely been a moment where I have
not been in love
In love with a person who despises me
Or soon will
As they all do in the end
But still I love
With every broken tendon of my heart I love
So to know I've never been loved at all is the
worst agony I've ever known

The Fall

I wait for the fall
Just as Lucifer foretold
From the pits of hell I have been raised up by the angel
In a story of old
Yet I wait again for the fall
For my wings to be cut brutally from my back
As they first were when I was merely a child
A child who looked to the heavens with awe
With clasped hands and prayers on her tongue
Now I look to the fallen angel to guide me
To guide me as I prepare for my inevitable descent
The descent into madness and strife
That's bane is so often love
For if there is one certainty in my human life
It is the fall

The Nightmare

It all begins to fade away like it's a bad dream
A mere nightmare
But it was my own personal hell
The screaming, the blood, the agony
My mind broken and my skin cut
I don't know how I survived
And yet now it seems little more than a bad
dream
Like some childhood story disappearing into
mere memory
Sometimes I have to look at what scars I can
find to convince myself it was real
That I was once bound in my own mortal hell
Most of my life I suffered in it
And now none of it feels real
Until I catch a glimpse of the devil in the mirror
Reminded it still lives within me
I it's home and it my hell
At last they are one and the same

Chains

I want love
But I know I won't find it here
And perhaps that's the greatest tragedy of all
Knowing no love I have will last
Until I leave this place forever
It once filled me with joy
The thought of escaping
Now I'm finding comfort in the chains of this
small town
In the permanence of all things
But I know if I do not leave now
Those chains will wrap themselves around my
throat
And I will never escape

The Death of a Poet

It is a strange thing
That all my favourite poets died by their own
hand
I read their words
Their every hope and sorrow
Knowing how it ends
Like a story already spoiled
Because there is no happy ending
For they all die in the end
Will I die also?
Will I die choking on fumes?
Or will I put rocks in my pockets and wade into
a lake?
Perhaps into the sea?
A true poet's death
Bidding my lover farewell
Knowing I'll see them again in the next life
For it is not death I fear
It is dying unloved that terrifies me most
For I live for love and little else
It would be a shame to die without it
In heartbreak I have become a poet
Just as all the greats
The human inheritance of agony and beauty